PHILOSOPHY

BULLET GUIDE

Robert Anderson

Hodder Education, 338 Euston Road, London NW1 3BH

Hodder Education is an Hachette UK company

First published in UK 2011 by Hodder Education

This edition published 2011

Copyright © 2011 Robert Anderson

The moral rights of the author have been asserted

Database right Hodder Education (makers)

Artworks (internal and cover): Peter Lubach

Cover concept design: Two Associates

British Library Cataloguing in Publication Data: a catalogue record for this title is available from the British Library.

10 9 8 7 6 5 4 3 2 1

The publisher has used its best endeavours to ensure that any website addresses referred to in this book are correct and active at the time of going to press. However, the publisher and the author have no responsibility for the websites and can make no guarantee that a site will remain live or that the content will remain relevant, decent or appropriate.

The publisher has made every effort to mark as such all words which it believes to be trademarks. The publisher should also like to make it clear that the presence of a word in the book, whether marked or unmarked, in no way affects its legal status as a trademark.

Every reasonable effort has been made by the publisher to trace the copyright holders of material in this book. Any errors or omissions should be notified in writing to the publisher, who will endeavour to rectify the situation for any reprints and future editions.

Hachette UK's policy is to use papers that are natural, renewable and recyclable products and made from wood grown in sustainable forests. The logging and manufacturing processes are expected to conform to the environmental regulations of the country of origin.

www.hoddereducation.co.uk

Typeset by Stephen Rowling/Springworks

Printed in Spain

For Maximilian

About the author

Robert Anderson is a freelance teacher, writer, editor and translator. He studied Modern Languages at the University of Exeter and went on to live in France for a number of years.

He has taught in schools in France and the United Kingdom and has worked in educational publishing for more than a decade. He has published a wide variety of children's and adult books, including a series of books on design icons for London's Design Museum as well as online courses for the Tate Gallery.

Acknowledgements

I would like to thank everyone at Hodder – especially Sam Richardson, Helen Rogers and Laura Davis – for their support (and patience!) during the writing of this book. My thanks also to David Porteous, David Price and Peter Lubach, editor, proofreader and illustrator respectively.

Robert Anderson
Scott Cottage, Roxburghshire, May 2011

Contents

Introduction

> **'The point of philosophy is to start with something so simple as not to seem worth stating, and to end with something so paradoxical that no one will believe it.'**
>
> Bertrand Russell

The British philosopher Russell's tongue-in-cheek jibe at his own profession will strike a chord with many. The very word 'philosophy' can provoke instantaneous disbelief, boredom, even fear. Philosophy's reputation for dry pedantry and self-reflexive argumentation is not helped by the tortured lives of one or two of its most famous practitioners – especially in the 'romantic' nineteenth century. **Friedrich Nietzsche** is the paradigm – spending the latter half of his life increasingly lonely and embittered before falling into 'madness' brought on by syphilis. Not the best advertisement for philosophy.

Read **Plato's dialogues** – the place where everyone curious about philosophy should begin – and you'll get a very different impression. Here philosophy is above all a sociable affair, a frank and lively exchange of opinions out in the fresh air or while reclining at a drinking party. The topics are all things we care about – love, friendship, courage… And when the conversation does get a little tougher, Plato helps us along with powerful, memorable metaphors. *This* philosophy is **profoundly human**.

Which is right – the 'good' view of philosophy or the bad one? The answer, of course, to take up Aristotle's idea of the Golden Mean, probably lies somewhere in the middle.

In this short introductory book, we'll first look at the question 'What is philosophy?' before tracing the **development of Western philosophical thought** since its earliest days in ancient Greece. Then we'll turn to the **three main branches of philosophy** – metaphysics, epistemology and ethics – before taking a final look at **philosophical methods**. The aim of this whistle-stop tour is to give you the basic outlines, to get you thinking, to get you involved in that lively conversation.

1 What is philosophy?

Preconceptions of philosophy

Philosophy need not be difficult, is rarely boring and really can shape the way we live our lives

Philosophy has a poor reputation. It's difficult, elitist, boring and, worst of all, irrelevant, isn't it? What, you ask, has philosophy got to do with ordinary life? It won't pay the bills, let alone solve global problems, will it? Isn't it just verbal nit-picking or, at best, a kind of super-sophisticated conversation for a select few 'in the know'?

This view of philosophy, however, is of relatively recent origin and, sadly, one that is especially prevalent in the Anglo-Saxon world. Philosophy need not be difficult (though, admittedly, it sometimes is), is rarely boring and really can shape the way we live our lives and even the course of human history.

Philosophy, moreover, is for everyone.

In this chapter we will look at:

* a few ideas on what philosophy might be about
* how the conception of philosophy has changed through history
* the big three philosophical questions
* the point of philosophy.

● Philosophy need not be difficult…

A few ideas

Defining philosophy is notoriously difficult. Let's start with a few reflections that philosophers themselves have made – sometimes with veneration, and sometimes, one suspects, in despair:

Philosophy begins in wonder.

Plato

What is the first business of philosophy? To part with self-conceit. For it is impossible for anyone to begin to learn what he thinks that he already knows.

Epictetus

To ridicule philosophy is really to philosophize.

Blaise Pascal

4

From these few examples, you might begin to characterize philosophy in the following ways:

* **wondering** why things are as they are
* aspiring to **knowledge** and 'digging deeper'
* questioning **habits of thought** or conventional ideas *and*
* running the risk of tying yourself in intellectual knots.

So what is philosophy?

A more succinct answer to the question 'What is philosophy?' is given in the renowned *The Oxford Companion to Philosophy*:

> *'Philosophy is thinking about thinking.'*

…but even as you contemplate this you may quickly begin to think you're trapped inside a hall of mirrors.

Changing conceptions

Part of the problem with defining philosophy is that its scope has changed considerably over time. Let's start with the ancient Greeks, with whom it arguably all began:

✳ The Greek word *philosophia* means **'love of wisdom'**. This sounds very broad, and indeed the earliest philosophers (the Presocratics) in ancient Greece asked some very broad questions about the nature of the world they saw around them, many of which we would today think of as **scientific**. Philosophy and science really only went separate ways with the development of the experimental method in the seventeenth century.

✳ During the Middle Ages (c. 500–1500), philosophy was a close companion of **theology** – the study of the nature of God and religion. Thus European philosophers, who at this time were often churchmen, looked at philosophical questions from a Christian viewpoint. Once again – in the West, at least – theology and philosophy began to diverge after the end of the Middle Ages, though the break was never as definitive as that between philosophy and science.

6

* The scope of philosophy in the modern era is therefore much narrower. Today philosophy has the reputation – only partly fairly – for being a somewhat insular and elitist **academic discipline**, a view encouraged by the fashionable (and ultimately self-defeating) 'in-house' conception of philosophy as a peculiar kind of 'language game' – a long way indeed from the 'wisdom' of ancient Greece.

However, in the following two sections, we'll go back to basics by:

* examining the principal questions of philosophy *and*
* asking what it's all for.

Part of the problem with defining philosophy is that its scope has changed considerably over time

The big three questions

Philosophy asks three principal questions:

1 what is the **nature of the world**?
2 how do we **know** anything?
3 how do we judge **what's right** and what's wrong?

These form the three main branches of philosophy:

1 metaphysics
2 epistemology
3 ethics.

None of these is really separate from the other. For example:

* what we can say about the nature of the world is dependent on what we know about it *and*
* what we consider to be our values for living well may well be dependent on what we think the nature of the world to be.

8

It can be useful to think of the branches of philosophy as forming a triangle:

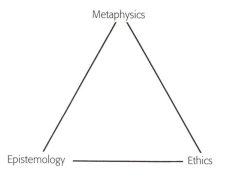

Figure 1.1: The three main branches of philosophy

The position you've taken on one of the branches will colour your view of the others.

We'll look again at each of the big three questions in the second half of the book.

Why philosophize?

'There is more wisdom in your body than in your deepest philosophy.'

Friedrich Nietzsche

Nietzsche, a philosopher himself of course, is making a valid point. Why philosophize at all? Why not just get on with the job of living, focus on the here and now? Asking the big questions may ultimately leave us feeling puzzled and stumped anyway.

Here are some possible retorts to Nietzsche:

* It's simply human nature to ask questions about why things are the way they are – the ability to philosophize, to reflect on our position (even our predicament), is what makes us human.
* Philosophy can make us, both as individuals and society, happier – thinking about what we really value can lead us to change the way we live.

* Philosophy can bring us closer to God (if we believe in one) – thinking about the nature of the world can deepen our feeling for the divine.
* Philosophy can change the world – you'll hardly need reminding that ideas can be powerful things. Plato's influence on the development of Western civilization is incalculable; Sartre's existentialism helped shape the liberation movements of the 1960s…

As you read through the rest of the book, try to keep asking yourself 'What's all this for?'

2 The ancient Greeks

The first philosophers

The origins of Western philosophy – like those of Western civilization more generally – are usually traced to the ancient Greeks. Other and earlier cultures had often pondered philosophical questions, of course, but the Greeks were the first to start developing sustained, systematic answers rooted both in **observation** of the external world and internally generated **rational argument**, or **logic**. They began the tradition and discipline of philosophical speculation that was passed on down through the generations.

The Greeks were the first to start developing sustained, systematic answers

The two giants of ancient Greek philosophy are **Plato** and **Aristotle**, whose copious writings have survived largely intact and whose ideas have resonated for two and a half thousand years.

In this chapter we will look at:

* the **Presocratics** – Socrates' immediate predecessors
* the philosophical enquiries of Plato known as the **dialogues**
* Plato's **Allegory of the Cave** – which has surely provided one of the most powerful metaphors or 'stories' in philosophy
* the encyclopaedic, ground-breaking work of Aristotle, especially his contribution to **logic**.

The Presocratics

In the sixth and fifth centuries BC a number of Greek thinkers began to reject mythological explanations for the universe and instead attempted to provide **rational theories** rooted in **direct observation**. The Presocratics tended to focus on two related questions:

1 What is the essence and **nature** of the world? (the **metaphysical** question)
2 How can we get to **know** the answers to such a question? (the **epistemological** question)

At this stage, what we now refer to as 'science' and 'philosophy' were part of the same intellectual project.

Key term: Presocratics
These early Greek philosophers are known as the Presocratics because they came *before* the Athenian philosopher Socrates who helped revolutionize philosophy in the fifth century BC. The ancient Greeks, however, called them *physiologoi*, or 'natural philosophers'.

The Presocratics came up with various answers to these questions.

What is the nature of the universe?

Everything changes and nothing remains still.

Heraclitus of Ephesus

Nothing changes.

Parmenides of Elea

The principles of mathematics are the root of all things.

Pythagoras of Samos

Everything is made up of atoms and has a material cause.

Democritis

How can we know anything?

We can gain knowledge only through reason, not sense perception.

Parmenides of Elea

Humans can only have an opinion of the truth, not truth itself.

Xenophanes of Colophon

Plato

The Athenian nobleman **Plato** (c. 428–347 BC) is undoubtedly the most influential thinker in the history of Western philosophy. He was a follower of **Socrates** (470–399 BC) whose execution by the Athenian state led Plato to abandon his career as a politician and devote himself to philosophy.

He wrote down his ideas in the form of **dialogues**, based on discussions between his real-life contemporaries, usually including Socrates in a starring role. In the earlier, 'Socratic' dialogues, the views expressed by Socrates in the dialogues seem to be closely modelled on those

> **Key term: dialectic**
> In the dialogues Plato has Socrates investigate philosophical issues by means of a process of questions and answers known as **dialectic**. By an exchange of opinion, participants are able to move closer to the truth. (For more on this, see Chapter 10.)

of the philosopher himself; in the later, 'Platonic' dialogues, Socrates is more of a mouthpiece for Plato.

The Socratic dialogues are usually quite short and focus generally on ethics (how should we live?). Key examples include:

* *Lysis* – what is friendship?
* *Laches* – what is courage?
* *Meno* – what is virtue?

The Platonic dialogues are often much more expansive – both in terms of length and the ambition of their ideas. The focus is often on **metaphysics** and **epistemology**. Key examples include:

* *Phaedo* – which shows Socrates preparing for death and arguing for the existence of an immortal soul
* *Republic* – a long series of dialogues discussing the nature of justice and the ideal city-state
* *Symposium* – where boozy participants at a drinking party discuss the nature of love.

The Allegory of the Cave

Plato's *Republic* includes one of the most influential ideas in Western history – and one that lies at the very heart of 'Platonic' philosophy. In this dialogue, Plato describes people chained to the wall of a cave who can only see the shadows cast on the wall by the real things outside the cave.

● 'If only we could get to see the real thing...'

This, for Plato, is an allegory of the **human condition**: the ultimate reality lies beyond the everyday, material world available to our senses.

The **job of the philosopher** is to offer insights into this ultimate reality.

The Allegory of the Cave is closely related to Plato's **theory of the Forms** (or Ideas):

＊ the Forms are the ultimate reality – the transcendental origin of the things we perceive in everyday life.

Or to put it the other way round:

＊ the things we see, touch, taste, etc., are transitory **representations** of ultimate realities.

Thus *this* book is just a temporary, shadowy expression of the ultimate Idea of the Book.

That we can recognize an individual object as an example of a general category (e.g. that we perceive a tree as a tree and not as an animal) is, for Plato, evidence for the existence of the Forms.

Plato's theory applies not just to objects but to acts as well – that we can recognize an act of courage suggests there is an ultimate Idea of courage. The highest Idea of all is **the Good**, which may or may not be divinity.

Aristotle

Aristotle (384–322 BC) studied under Plato for almost 20 years, after which he famously acted as tutor to Alexander the Great. Aristotle wrote about an **encyclopaedic range** of what today we would take to be philosophical, scientific and cultural subjects.

His major works include:

* *Metaphysics* – the study of 'first philosophy' or 'the study of being as being'
* *Nicomachean Ethics* – an investigation into the fundamentals of moral philosophy
* *Politics* – a study of the ethics of human affairs – i.e. political philosophy (*polis* = 'city' in Greek)
* *Organon* – a six-volume manual on logic.

● 'I'm going to read every bit of Aristotle.'

With these mammoth tomes, Aristotle launched some of the great themes of Western philosophy.

CASE STUDY: Logic

In one of the volumes in the *Organon*, Aristotle pioneered the use of **formal logic** in philosophy. In particular, he established the **syllogism** – logical argument by inference – as the fundamental principle of logical argument.

The most basic syllogism runs as follows:

if all A's are B (major premise)

and all B's are C (minor premise)

then all A's are C (conclusion)

So, to take the most famous syllogism:

if all men are mortal

and all Greeks are men

then all Greeks are mortal

For Aristotle, the syllogism was a **vital tool** for the philosopher as he ploughed his way towards the truth.

3 Medieval Christendom

Faith seeking understanding

Christian thinkers of the medieval period (c. fifth to fifteenth century) used philosophy to **deepen understanding of their faith**. They were churchmen themselves – bishops, friars, priests and so on – for whom philosophy (the pursuit of wisdom) and **theology** (the science of God) were the same, or at least working companions. In the words of St Anselm, Christian philosophy was 'faith in search of understanding'.

Christian philosophy was 'faith in search of understanding'

Nonetheless medieval philosophers revered the works of the ancient Greek philosophers deeply – especially

Aristotle, whom they referred to simply as 'the Philosopher'. They strove to show how Christianity not only did not contradict, but could be bolstered by, ancient philosophy and its emphasis on rationality. Belief in God did not require a leap of blind faith – it was a matter of logic.

In this chapter we will look at:

* the work of St Augustine, who acted as a kind of bridge between the classical and medieval worlds
* the relationship between faith and reason
* St Thomas Aquinas and five proofs for the existence of God
* the great medieval debate between realists and nominalists.

St Augustine

St Augustine (354–430) was the bridge between ancient and medieval philosophy. As a young man he was steeped in classical culture, especially the **Neoplatonic thinkers** of late antiquity (who, as their name suggests, took their inspiration from Plato). Augustine embraced Christianity at the age of 31 and thereafter devoted himself to a life of reflection and writing. In 395 he became bishop of Hippo (now in Algeria).

Augustine's most famous and influential works are:

* *Confessions* – a spiritual autobiography
* *The City of God* (413–26) – a vast treatise on human history as the working out of God's divine plan.

Throughout his works, the spirit of Plato is never far away: Augustine's God draws close to the Greek philosopher's Idea of the Good – as the highest, ultimate source of all things.

CASE STUDY: The problem of evil

One of Augustine's most famous philosophical arguments concerns the problem of evil. As a young man Augustine had been a follower of **Manichaeism**, a religion that believed the world was made up of a mixture of good and evil. As a Christian, Augustine found this viewpoint abhorrent. His argument ran like this:

* God is good
* God is the ultimate source of all things
* how then do we explain evil – the 'bad' things that happen in the world?
* evil, in fact, is not a thing at all but a nothing – a 'falling away' from God and the Good.

This kind of argument about the problem of evil and the nature of God is known as a **theodicy**.

Faith and reason

Medieval philosophers, and the age they lived in, have a reputation for obscurity, irrationality and pedantry – for arguing about 'how many angels could dance on a needle'.

Look at some famous quotes by some of the greatest thinkers of the Middle Ages and ask yourself whether you think this reputation is fair.

> The truth can be perceived only through thinking, as proved by Augustine.

Thomas Aquinas

> It is futile to do with more things that which can be done with fewer.

William of Ockham

> Nor do I seek to understand that I may believe, but I believe that I may understand. For this, too, I believe, that, unless I first believe, I shall not understand.

Anselm of Canterbury

While there are plenty of examples of obscurity and absurdity in medieval philosophy, the central concern of medieval philosophy was with how **reason** could illuminate **faith**, and vice versa. Medieval philosophy, especially when viewed on its own terms, is remarkably rigorous and clear-eyed.

The philosophy of the Middle Ages is often known as **scholasticism**, since it arose from the monastic 'schools' or universities. Rather than being a particular philosophical world view, it was closer to being a method or approach to philosophy.

Scholasticism can be characterized by:

* its emphasis on **dialectic** – the progression of knowledge through rigorous questions and answers
* its use of **Aristotelian logic** – extending knowledge by deduction
* the **reconciliation** of classical and Christian views.

Proving the existence of God

St Thomas Aquinas (1225–74) was the most influential philosopher of the Middle Ages. His thought was in essence an ongoing **dialogue with the ideas of Aristotle** and an attempt to show how Christian ideas about God – indeed His very existence – arise from 'natural reason'. His major work is the ***Summa Theologiae*** (Compendium of Theology; 1265–74).

Five proofs for the existence of God

Aquinas used Aristotelian logic to prove the existence of God in five ways – the so-called *Quinque Viae* (Five Ways):

1 The **Argument of the Unmoved Mover** – things move because something else has caused them to move; however, there cannot be an infinite chain of cause and effect; therefore there must have been something that caused the first movement – i.e. that which we call God.

2 The **Argument of the First Cause** – closely related to (1) is the argument that in the chain of cause and effect there must be a First Cause.

3 The **Argument from Contingency** – everything in the world has the possibility of either existing or not existing (i.e. is contingent); there must be something that is absolutely necessary (i.e. not contingent) – i.e. God.

4 The **Argument from Degree** – everything is more or less good than something else; this presupposes that there must be something that is most good – i.e. God.

5 The **Argument of the Intelligent Designer** – everything has a purpose (even if it is unaware of that purpose), so there must be an intelligent being who gave things their purpose.

Aquinas's arguments have had a tough time at the hands of atheists – and it's probably not hard to see why.

The great medieval debate

Medieval philosophers debated many things, but one philosophical problem that provoked a great deal of argument was that of the **universals**.

* In Chapter 2 we saw how Plato argued for the existence of Forms or Ideas, transcendental universals that correspond to particular examples of not just tangible **objects,** such as dogs and cats, but also to the **qualities** of things, such as beauty and goodness. Doghood, Cathood, Beauty, Truth and so on are ultimate **realities**, not figments of our minds. For this reason, this philosophical standpoint is known as **realism**.

An important proponent of realism was the Scottish Franciscan **John Duns Scotus** (c. 1266–1308).

* The opposing viewpoint – which denies the existence of universals – is known as **nominalism**. Nominalists argue that categories of objects and general qualities exist only in our minds and are merely the **names** (hence the term 'nominalism') that we give to things to

classify phenomena. They are just words or conceptual conveniences, while the world is really made up of just **individual things**.

CASE STUDY: William of Ockham

The key medieval exponent of nominalism was the English Franciscan friar William of Ockham (1285–1347). For Ockham, philosophical theories had to be based on the simplest of presuppositions (this is the famous principle still known as **Ockham's razor**), while the existence of universals had a strong mystical quality that he shied away from.

On first sight the argument about universals can seem obscure – a stereotypical example of medieval obscurantism. In reality, it spoke to enduring questions of philosophy: to what extent (if at all) does the world exist beyond our individual minds? – and from what or from where does knowledge derive?

4 The Enlightenment

Empiricism

For the empiricists the human mind and human experience played the starring role

In the seventeenth century the English thinkers Francis Bacon and John Locke developed a radical view of the **nature of knowledge**, arguing that human ideas all have their origin in sense impressions – that is, in our experience of the world around us. This standpoint is known as **empiricism**.

The origins of empiricism can be traced back to earlier ideas such as nominalism. However, the English empiricists argued their case with a new forcefulness, seemingly turning philosophy on its head. While much earlier philosophy had placed God or some other transcendental subject at centre stage, for the empiricists the human mind and human experience played the starring role.

Empiricism shaped the ideas of the Enlightenment – the so-called **Age of Reason** of the eighteenth century.

In this chapter we will look at:

* Locke's ideas about knowledge as reflected in his *Essay Concerning Human Understanding*
* the key ideas that underpinned the Enlightenment
* the contributions of David Hume and Immanuel Kant.

Another early influence on Enlightenment philosophy was the Frenchman René Descartes (1596–1650), who is responsible for the most famous philosophical sound bite ever: ***cogito ergo sum*** (I think therefore I am).

John Locke – understanding knowledge

John Locke's *Essay Concerning Human Understanding* (1690) is a kind of blueprint of Enlightenment thought. In it, he argued that:

* human beings are born with no inherent ideas or knowledge – they are like sheets of **'white paper'**
* we derive **simple ideas** – e.g. the roundness of a ball, the sweetness of sugar – through experience
* through the powers of reason we use these simple ideas to develop **complex ideas** such as abstractions, number, identity, comparison and so on
* this body of complex ideas is **knowledge**.

● Locke would say that experience makes us what we are and gives us what we think…

40

Locke's political philosophy also deeply influenced Enlightenment thought about the relationship between the **State and the individual**. The key work here is *The Two Treatises of Government* (1690).

In Locke's view, 'in the state of nature' human beings lived freely and **reasonably** without rulers or authority. Later, people agreed to accept government from above, though only in order to promote their mutual duty not to 'harm one another in his life… liberty, or goods'.

On the basis of his view of human nature and society, Locke:

* rejected the idea that power was bestowed by God (e.g. the Renaissance concept of the 'Divine Right of Kings')
* argued that power was conferred only by **'the will and determination of the majority'**.

Locke's ideas had a powerful impact on the development of **liberal democracy** (and also free-market capitalism).

What is Enlightenment?

In 1784 the German philosopher **Immanuel Kant** published an essay called 'An Answer to the Question: What is Enlightenment?'. He summed up his answer thus:

'Enlightenment is man's emergence from his self-incurred immaturity.'

Kant went on to explain exactly what he meant by **immaturity**:

'...the inability to use one's own understanding without the guidance of others.'

For a **moral or intellectual compass**, the enlightened, mature individual – and by extension the enlightened society – relied not on the teachings of tradition or the authority of the Church and State but on the **self**.

Kant summed up his belief in the motto: 'Dare to know!'

Generally speaking, the Enlightenment philosophers:

* rejected scholasticism and the **dogmas of the Church**
* gave pride of place to human **reason**
* questioned the **power of the State**
* championed the **freedom** of the individual
* were often **atheistic** or **agnostic** and **anti-theological**.

The Enlightenment philosophers, of course, had a wide range of ideas and, naturally enough given their philosophical stance, often disagreed with one another vehemently. *En masse*, however, their ideas and values – and the intellectual ferment they inspired – had a powerful impact on human history.

The limits of reason

While the Enlightenment, as we've seen, is often characterized as the Age of Reason, many of its philosophers were in fact concerned with the **limitations** of reason. The most important figure in this respect is the Scottish thinker **David Hume** (1711–76), whose key work is *A Treatise of Human Nature* (1739–40).

Hume argued that reason alone is unable to account for everything that we believe about the world. For example:

* we believe that objects dropped from a building will always fall
* however, just because we may have experienced a particular object falling from a building does not necessarily mean that we can infer a universal rule that *all* things dropped from buildings fall *for all time*
* the 'reason' we believe this to be the case is in fact sheer **habit** – the accumulation of repeated experiences of objects falling – and habit is **not reason**.

44

Hume and morality

Hume's scepticism about the power of reason also extends to **morality**. He argued that we decide what is right or wrong not on the basis of thinking through an action logically, but because we **feel** it to be the case – that is, on the basis of a 'moral sense'.

'Morals excite passions, and produce or prevent actions. Reason itself is utterly impotent in this particular. The rules of morality, therefore, are not conclusions of our reason.'

David Hume

It's worth comparing Hume's view of morality with that of Kant. Which do you find most convincing?

Immanuel Kant

Immanuel Kant (1724–1804) is often considered to be both the greatest of Enlightenment philosophers and the first of the 'modern' philosophers. His best-known works are:

* *Critique of Pure Reason* (1781, revised 1787)
* *Critique of Practical Reason* (1788).

Kant argued that empirical evidence – the evidence of our senses – sets a **limit** on what we can reasonably philosophize about. Thus we cannot prove or disprove the existence of God or a soul.

However, he later also argued that, for us to make any sense of our lives, we have to **postulate** a god – that is, assume one exists.

46

CASE STUDY: The categorical imperative

Kant also developed a powerful and influential ethical philosophy. Morality was hitherto largely derived from religious or conventional teachings – e.g. the biblical Ten Commandments. Kant, by contrast, argued that the morality of any particular action could be derived by the individual using their own powers of reason.

This involved a sort of test under which you ask yourself whether you would want your act to become a **universal law**. For example:

✳ It is right for me to lie about having borrowed a friend's car…
✳ …so it is OK to lie when it suits your interests to do so.

This, Kant would argue, is unreasonable: if everybody lied, then lying itself would have no meaning as it depends on people telling the truth most of the time. Immoral acts are therefore, logically speaking, self-contradictory. Kant called this moral law the **categorical imperative**.

5 Modern philosophy

Beginning afresh

By the second half of the nineteenth century and into the twentieth, there was the growing sense that the traditional preoccupations of philosophy were becoming seriously out of kilter with the rapidly changing industrialized societies of Europe and North America due to:

* the ascendancy of the **scientific world view** (e.g. the evolutionary theories of Charles Darwin) which appeared to push metaphysical enquiry to the sidelines
* **political and social developments** – urbanization, democratization, etc. – which made conventional philosophy seem increasingly remote and 'irrelevant' to the lives of ordinary people
* growing **scepticism** about the **Christian faith**.

The traditional preoccupations of philosophy were becoming seriously out of kilter with the rapidly changing industrialized societies of Europe and North America

To keep up with the times, philosophy had, arguably, to reinvent itself and reconnect with the world.

In this chapter we will look at:

* Friedrich Nietzsche – the key figure in the forging of modern philosophy
* Ludwig Wittgenstein and the *Tractatus Logico-Philosophicus*
* the existentialists
* postmodernism and the 'death' of philosophy.

God is dead!

Friedrich Nietzsche

Nietzsche – a new philosophy

The German philosopher **Friedrich Nietzsche** (1844–1900) has a poor reputation. Pessimistic, mad and bad, he was undoubtedly a key influence on the Nazis. Yet his thought also marks a key moment in the development of philosophy, sweeping away what he considered to be the 'other-worldly' obsessions of earlier philosophers and dragging the discipline into the here and now.

Let's begin with what Nietzsche vigorously denounced:

* ideas of a transcendental, **'higher' reality**, including the notion of a god
* the 'slave' **morality** espoused by Christianity
* **absolute ideas** about 'truth' and 'knowledge' (but not the very existence of truth and knowledge).

For Nietzsche, these were all simply comforting illusions that disable us from living full and fulfilling lives.

The reality of the world, he surmised, is that it is **irrational** and

meaningless – an arena of competing energies, a place of struggle and suffering. This sounds bleak, but Nietzsche also throws us a **lifeline**:

* a clear-sighted **acceptance of the world as it is**
* the creation of new, life-affirming (not life-denying) values – a **'master' morality**
* a devotion to **self-expression** and the transformation of the world.

The *Übermensch*

Such ideas crystallized in the idea of the *Übermensch* – the 'superior person' who lives creatively and energetically, who strives for a 'higher humanity', and who asserts himself against the 'mediocre' masses. Here Nietzsche seems to be a prophet for the **individualism** that has been such a hallmark of modern culture. Sadly, it is also not hard to see how Hitler found such woeful justification in the philosopher's ideas for his **genocidal racial policies**.

Wittgenstein

Philosophers are famous for being verbose. The Austrian philosopher **Ludwig Wittgenstein** (1889–1951) published just one 75-page book in his lifetime – the *Tractatus Logico-Philosophicus* (1921), made up of a series of numbered, compact and seemingly mysterious sentences. These range from the opening proposition:

'The world is all that is the case.'

…to what is perhaps the most famous of Wittgenstein's dictums:

'What we cannot speak about we must pass over in silence.'

Despite its brevity the *Tractatus* revolutionized what might be called the philosophical project by arguing:

✳ all that can be said about the traditional questions of philosophy – about ethics and religion, for example – is simply a linguistic nonsense

* philosophy is not a science
* the goal of philosophy is to decide what *can* and *cannot* be expressed philosophically in terms of language.

Wittgenstein's short book was as revolutionary in its way as Einstein's General Theory of Relativity (1916). His goal was nothing less than to destroy philosophy as traditionally understood so as to enable it to begin afresh. Even the *Tractatus* was senseless:

> My propositions are elucidatory in this way: he who understands me finally recognizes them as senseless, when he has climbed out through them, on them, over them. (He must so to speak throw away the ladder, after he has climbed up on it.) He must surmount these propositions; then he sees the world rightly.

Existentialism

As its name implies, existentialism is concerned with **human existence**, focusing on the key question: 'How should we live?' As we've seen, this has been an abiding concern of philosophy since ancient times. However, in the twentieth century a group of French philosophers – led by Jean-Paul Sartre (1905–80), Simone de Beauvoir (1908–86) and Albert Camus (1913–60) – aimed to forge a philosophy that would have a direct, powerful impact both on **individual lives** and on the **political direction** of society more generally.

Sartre argued that:

* Humans are alone in having the freedom to choose what we do or what we do not do.
* In this sense, we do not have a **given nature** (we are a kind of 'nothing', to use Sartre's terminology) but **become** what we choose to be. Sartre summed up this idea in the famous maxim: 'Man's existence precedes his essence.'

✳ This freedom can be both a liberation and a burden – we alone have responsibility for our lives.

'We are condemned to be free.'

Jean-Paul Sartre

Such ideas – expressed not only in weighty, theory-laden tomes but also in accessible novels and plays – had a powerful impact on generations of students and young people in the wake of World War II. Existentialism seemed to offer both a **philosophy for individualism** and a **programme for political change**. Crucially, existentialist thinkers like Sartre and de Beauvoir were also political activists.

The Outsider

The most famous existentialist novel is Camus's *L'Étranger* (The Outsider) – the story of a white French-Algerian who murders an Arab and is then sentenced to death.

Postmodernism

Postmodernism is a notoriously tricky term to define but in terms of philosophy it might be said to have the following broad characteristics:

* there is **no single, absolute truth** – truth is multiple, fractured and 'slippery'
* knowledge is essentially about **power** – a 'discourse' deployed by those who wish to maintain power over others
* philosophy does not offer a privileged, unbiased insight into truth but is itself an example of a **discourse**
* philosophy is essentially a **'language game'**.

Postmodern philosophers often take an explicitly **anti-Enlightenment** stance and attack humanist ideas about 'reason' and 'morality'. We can see such 'postmodernist' thoughts already in action in the work of Nietzsche and Wittgenstein.

CASE STUDY: Richard Rorty

The American philosopher Richard Rorty (1931–2007) is a key figure in postmodern philosophy. In his 1979 book *Philosophy and the Mirror of Nature* he argued that ever since Plato philosophy has been based on the fallacy that it is possible to achieve an **objective** or **final view** of the world.

Instead, he argued philosophy has in fact always been just a temporary, convenient but ultimately misleading way of talking about the world at a particular time and place. In this view, the philosopher is (at best) little more than a **sophisticated conversationalist**.

In this view, philosophy seems to be simply a dead end, seemingly closing off the mouth of Plato's cave and leaving us only to admire the shadows.

6 Non-Western philosophy

Eastern inspirations

Conventional histories of philosophy more often than not exclude non-Western traditions of ethical and metaphysical thought, thereby creating a straightforward, discrete narrative that begins with the Greeks and then progresses, seemingly entirely under its own steam, up until the present day.

Nonetheless the philosophical traditions of **Asia** and the **Near East** are rich and illuminating in their own right, often offering fresh perspectives on the enduring questions of their European counterpart.

Moreover, Western philosophy is not so self-sufficient as the conventional 'grand narrative' would suggest. Thus, for example, Islamic philosophy, which itself grew out of the ideas of ancient Greece, was a vital influence on the Christian thinkers of the Middle Ages.

The philosophical traditions of Asia and the Near East are rich and illuminating... offering fresh perspectives on the enduring questions of their European counterpart

In this chapter we will look at:

* the Vedic philosophy of ancient India
* the Islamic philosophy of Ibn Sīnā (Avicenna)
* the ethical teachings of the Chinese thinker Confucius
* some modern non-Western philosophers.

Vedic philosophy

The ancient Indian scriptures known as the **Vedas** (c. 1500 BC to 400 BC) provide one of the earliest bodies of philosophical thought and were the origin of a large number of competing schools of Hindu philosophy.

One of the key Vedic texts was the **Upanishads**, the oldest of which were composed around 900 BC. At its core are two key principles:

1 **brahman** – the universal spirit which is the origin and basis of the universe
2 **ātman** – the Self or individual spirit.

Over hundreds of years Indian philosophers debated the exact relationship between these two. The main argument was between…

* **Monist philosophers**, notably Śankara (788–820), who argued that ātman and brahman are **identical**. The external world of multiple things is an illusion; everything is pure consciousness, leading to the Vedic dictums 'You are that' and 'I am all that exists'. (Descartes springs to mind!)

and…

* **Dualist philosophers**, notably Madhava (thirteenth century), who argued that the world has an independent reality and is infinitely divisible, and that ātman and brahman are separate.

The **mystical aphorisms** commonplace in Indian philosophy influenced Western philosophers such as Wittgenstein.

As you read through this chapter, think about how the ideas of non-Western philosophies might relate to ideas you have read about in earlier chapters.

Confucius and Confucianism

Chinese philosophy has traditionally been concerned with **practical issues**, such as how to live well and the ideal political state, rather than with metaphysical speculation. The foundational figure is **Confucius** (Chinese: *K'ung Ch'iu*), who lived around the turn of the sixth and fifth centuries BC. His sayings were collected in a book called the *Analects*.

The late Chou dynasty during which Confucius lived was a period of social and political turmoil and his philosophy thus aimed at helping to restore harmony. Confucius recommended:

* an ethics based on **concern for others**
* the practice of **ceremonious behaviour** – such as the welcoming of guests into the home
* a political philosophy based on the idea of the **ruler acting as a virtuous model** for his subjects.

66

The Golden Rule

Confucian ethics can be summed up in his 'golden maxim': 'Never impose on others what you would not choose for yourself.' This 'rule' – found widely in traditional societies – amounts to a kind of enlightened self-interest.

The early dialogues of Plato show a similar concern with social virtues. However, the *Analects*…

* are **prescriptive** not discursive – i.e. they offer a list of desirable behaviours
* do not deploy a **philosophical method** (compare the question-and-answer format of the Socratic dialogue)
* do not have **a metaphysical dimension**.

For these reasons, from a Western perspective, Confucianism is arguably closer to being a kind of moral code rather than a full-blown 'philosophy'. Perhaps its very practicality has ensured that it has remained a powerful influence on Chinese society right up until the present day.

Ibn Sīnā

Like his close contemporary Thomas Aquinas, the Persian Islamic thinker Ibn Sīnā (980–1037) – known in the West by his Latinized name, **Avicenna** – was concerned with how to reconcile classical Greek philosophy with the theology of his religion. His philosophical writings helped to establish Aristotle as the key influence on medieval philosophy, in both the Islamic and Christian worlds.

Ibn Sīnā was a highly **original** philosopher – indeed, much more so than his Christian contemporaries. One of his key ideas was the distinction between three types of entity:

1 the **impossible** (e.g. a square circle)
2 the **possible** or contingent (all the things in the world) *and*
3 the **necessary**.

Ibn Sīnā equated the idea of the **Necessary Being** with God, who is the first cause of all other entities.

CASE STUDY: The 'floating man'

The 'floating man' thought experiment is one of Ibn Sīnā's most famous philosophical arguments:

* imagine God instantly creates a grown-up man floating in mid-air with all his limbs outstretched and wearing a blindfold
* he has no awareness of having a body
* nonetheless he is aware of his own existence as an individual thing
* from this we can deduce that the body and the 'soul' (or 'mind') are, potentially at least, two distinct concepts.

This idea – of **an affirmation of existence** dependent on mind alone – looks forward in some respects to Descartes's famous dictum: *cogito ergo sum* (I think therefore I am).

Modern non-Western philosophers

During the twentieth century many non-Western philosophers have often sought to use Western ideas and terminology to elucidate and extend their native traditions. Some outstanding examples, together with their key works, include:

Nishida Kitaro (1870–1945)

Japanese thinker who developed a philosophy rooted in Zen Buddhism and the Western thinkers Henri Bergson and William James.

Key work: *An Inquiry into the Good* (1911)

Sarvepalli Radhakrishnan (1888–1975)

Indian thinker and politician who served as Indian's president from 1962 to 1967. A monist, he sought to find (and build) bridges between classical Indian and Western philosophies.

Key work: *An Idealist View of Life* (1929)

> ## 'Books are the means by which we build bridges between cultures.'
> Sarvepalli Radhakrishnan

Fazlur Rahman Malik
(1919–88)

Pakistani thinker who argued for a revival of the intellectual dynamism of classical Islamic philosophy.

Key work: *Islam*
(2nd edition; 1979)

Kwame Gyekye
(1939–)

Ghanaian thinker who argues for an explicitly African philosophy based on the individual living in harmony with the community and God.

Key work: *The Unexamined Life: Philosophy and the African Experience* (1988)

7 Metaphysics

'Beyond physics'

In the following three chapters we will look at the three big questions of philosophy. Here's a reminder:

1 what is the **nature of the world**? (metaphysics)
2 how do we **know** anything? (epistemology)
3 how do we judge **what's right** and what's wrong? (ethics)

We'll begin with metaphysics – the most **abstract** of the three main kinds of philosophy. Metaphysics deals with 'ultimate reality'. What really lies at the foundation of the world? God, matter, consciousness…? In what sense do things exist?

● How do we know anything?

Metaphysics is a vast and intricate subject and we can only highlight a small number of its concerns here.

In this chapter we will look at:

* the problem of free will
* the mind and matter problem
* philosophical objections to metaphysics.

Key term: metaphysics
Metaphysics literally means 'beyond physics', though not in the sense that its scope is beyond the realm of physics. It got its name because Aristotle's treatment of metaphysical questions followed on from ('was beyond') his book *Physics*.

Determinism and free will

The philosophical idea that everything in the world is an effect caused by an earlier effect – that is, is governed by an unbreakable chain of cause and effect – is known as **determinism**. The American philosopher William James (1842–1910) described this graphically as the 'iron block universe'.

The problem determinism poses for human beings is that it would seem to exclude the possibility of **free will** – that is, our freedom to shape the future. Philosophers have responded to this issue in radically different ways:

1 **Hard determinists** argue that free will is merely an illusion and human beings are condemned to take their place as cogs in a universal machine.

76

2 **Compatibilists** argue that free will and determinism are compatible – the German thinker Arthur Schopenhauer (1788–1860) famously declared: 'Man can do what he wills but he cannot will what he wills.' On this understanding, the concept of free will has a kind of *superficial* truth.

3 **Hard incompatibilists** insist there is neither determinism nor free will – humans exist in a chaotic universe over which they have no control.

4 **Libertarians** deny determinism, but allow humans free will.

The problem of free will has vital repercussions for ethics: if we have no free will, how can we be held responsible for our acts?

The problem of free will has vital repercussions for ethics...

Dualism

Are mind and matter – the latter including, notably, the body – two different kinds of substance, or are they really the same thing? This is a problem that has taxed philosophers since ancient times. Many have taken a **dualist** (two-substance) point of view:

* Plato distinguished between the material body and the 'soul', which belonged to the realm of **the Forms**
* Ibn Sīnā's famous **'floating man'** thought experiment supported the idea of two substances
* in the seventeenth century the French philosopher Descartes's famous **proof for his own existence** also suggested (but did not prove) that body and mind were *probably* distinct and separate (although he also believed they could influence each other)…
  » I can doubt that I have a body – after all, it could be an illusion
  » but I cannot doubt that I have a mind – how else otherwise could I think that thought?
  » so *cogito ergo sum* – 'I think therefore I am'.

Mind over matter

Mind–body dualism – evident not only in Platonic and **Cartesian** (relating to the ideas of Descartes) but also in Christian thought – has had a powerful impact on Western civilization, since it has tended to give a privileged place to the mind or soul over the body.

For instance, with the body demoted to a second-class citizen, sex becomes a source of anxiety rather than pleasure. Similarly, vision – with the eyes conceived as 'windows of the soul' – takes priority over the other, more 'embodied' senses, such as touch and smell.

Idealists and materialists
Thought is merely the residue of sensations of the world acting upon our bodies

Other philosophers have come up with radically different solutions to the mind–matter problem, and we can divide them into idealists and materialists. Both solutions, however, deny there is any split between the two at all:

* **Idealists** argue that ultimately all matter is *nothing but mind*. For example, for an idealist the existence of a dog rests entirely on our perception of certain attributes of dogginess – it barks, it has a waggy tail and so on.

George Berkeley
The Anglo-Irish philosopher George Berkeley (1685–1753) summed up the idealist position, which he called 'immaterialism', in the Latin phrase ***esse est percipi*** (to be is to be perceived).

✳ **Materialists** argue the opposite case: everything, including mind, is *nothing but matter*. Human beings have no souls and our minds are just the interaction of the brain with the physical world.

Thomas Hobbes

The best known of the materialist philosophers is the Englishman Thomas Hobbes (1588–1678), whose major work is *Leviathan* (1651). There he argued that the world is entirely made up of matter in motion and that thought is merely the residue of sensations of the world acting upon our bodies.

'...and the life of man, solitary, poor, nasty, brutish and short.'

Thomas Hobbes

Against metaphysics

Some philosophers as well as many non-philosophers have rejected metaphysics entirely. Here are the words of two prominent refuseniks:

> *If we take in our hand any volume; of divinity or school metaphysics, for instance; let us ask, Does it contain any abstract reasoning concerning quantity or number? No. Does it contain any experimental reasoning concerning matter of fact and existence? No. Commit it then to the flames: for it can contain nothing but sophistry and illusion.*

David Hume

> *Metaphysics is a dark ocean without shores or lighthouse, strewn with many a philosophic wreck.*

Immanuel Kant

The essential objection to metaphysical ideas is *either*:

* that they are **unverifiable** in empirical terms (i.e. through the senses)

or (a more recent objection)

* that they are **linguistically nonsense** – words tying themselves up in knots

or (a layman's objection)

* that they are simply too technical and useless.

What do you think about metaphysics? Are these criticisms fair? Do ideas have to be verifiable – philosophy, after all, is not a science...

8 Epistemology

Knowledge theory

Epistemology is philosophical enquiry into the **nature of knowledge** (*episteme* is the ancient Greek word for 'knowledge').

> **Without some kind of reasonably firm theory of knowledge, we are liable to end up in philosophical quicksand**

Common sense might tell us that knowledge is just the **accumulation of facts about the world**: $3 + 2 = 5$, elephants are mammals, and so on. But what qualifies something to count as a fact? Do these facts exist independently of us or are they in some sense derived from our minds? If the former, how do these facts *enter* our minds as knowledge? Philosophers have puzzled over all these and many other epistemological questions.

Epistemology is **fundamental** to all other kinds of philosophy. If we are to draw closer to any kind of truth about the world, we need to acquire an understanding of how we can know anything about it. Without some kind of reasonably firm theory of knowledge, we are liable to end up in philosophical quicksand.

In this chapter we will look at:

* a simple definition of what knowledge might be
* different ways in which knowledge might be acquired
* the philosophical tradition of scepticism
* practical applications of epistemology.

What is knowledge?

For thousands of years philosophers have pretty much agreed on what knowledge is:

$$\boxed{\text{knowledge} = \text{belief} + \text{truth}}$$

Let's unpick this short equation:

* **Belief** is an individual's 'take' on the world, but beliefs are not necessarily true – e.g. 'I believe in my doctor' is a statement of personal faith not knowledge.
* To be **true**, we have to offer some external fact condition to back it up – e.g. I believe the sky is blue (because I and others can *see* it is blue) = I know the sky is blue.

Some philosophers have gone a little further and added another element to the equation:

$$\boxed{\text{knowledge} = \text{belief} + \text{truth} + \text{justification}}$$

＊ To know something we have to have **good reason** to believe something to be true – e.g. I know this bridge is safe because I have just crossed over it. (*Before* I crossed it I merely believed it to be true by all appearances.)

Edmund Gettier
In the 1960s the American philosopher Edmund Gettier (1927–) threw a spanner into the works by arguing that justified true beliefs were not quite enough to define knowledge because of the possibility of coincidence or luck. That bridge you crossed might not be safe at all – you just *happened* to step on the right planks!

Acquiring knowledge

We may know what knowledge is, but how do we acquire it? There are two main tendencies:

1 **Empiricism** – knowledge is acquired through our senses – i.e. through our interaction with the world. **Sense data** is the basic ingredient of knowledge here.
2 **Idealism** – knowledge is innate – i.e. it is embedded in the pre-existing structure of our minds. *Or* it exists as part of an eternal 'higher reality' (e.g. Plato's theory of the Forms).

The empirical and idealist tendencies are not mutually exclusive: some kinds of knowledge might be empirical, some ideal.

> **Key terms: a priori and a posteriori**
> The distinction between ideal and empirical knowledge is often cast in the form of a distinction between **a priori** (prior to) knowledge and **a posteriori** (afterwards) knowledge.

CASE STUDY: The philosophy of maths

What kind of knowledge is mathematics then? This question was a subject for debate among the ancient Greeks. Here is Plato's argument:

* numbers are **perfect** – i.e. each is a unit that is perfectly equal to every other unit
* such perfect units do not exist in the everyday world we know
* therefore they belong to a **different world** – the world of pure intelligence or the Forms
* and since we cannot know numbers through experience our knowledge of them must be **a priori**.

This view of mathematics has often been challenged – Plato's pupil Aristotle, for example, argued the rather more down-to-earth view that numbers can in fact be related to real objects, as found in the classroom arithmetic of apples and pears.

Scepticism

Can we really have knowledge of anything? A powerful and ancient tradition in philosophy has doubted that all or at least some kinds of knowledge are possible to acquire. This is the argument of **scepticism**.

> ### 'I know nothing except the fact of my ignorance.'
> Socrates (as 'quoted' by Diogenes Laertius)

This Socratic statement argues that scepticism is a **good basis for philosophy**. By beginning with doubt and questioning received 'knowledge' we have a much better chance of getting at the truth. This is the method that underpins the dialogues (see Chapter 2).

● It's wise to feel ignorant…

92

A slightly later Greek philosopher, Pyrrho of Elis, took scepticism to an extreme: in his view you should **doubt everything** and suspend judgement. Such a viewpoint, however, threatens to undermine philosophy entirely rather than nurture it.

The **destructive power** of the sceptical viewpoint has disturbed many philosophers, who have tried to refute it and thereby gain a stable foundation for knowledge. Descartes began by playing devil's advocate:

* what if all I experience is simply a dream?
* what if I am the victim of the delusions of an evil demon?

In the face of such overwhelming, all-encompassing doubt, Descartes fought back, acquiring **certainties** one after the other:

* the existence of the mind (the 'I think therefore I am' argument)
* the existence of God…

Most philosophers are not quite sure he succeeded in his project!

Applications of epistemology

Philosophy has a reputation for being impractical, even useless; epistemology, like ethics, is a good example of the opposite point of view. Here are a few areas where the philosophy of knowledge is often applied or has practical value:

* **archaeology** – how can we derive knowledge of the past from fragments and ruins?
* **law** – how should we determine guilt?
* **medicine** – how should we diagnose disease?
* **product testing** – how can we be sure that a product won't fail?

Should we make judgements in such areas based solely on empirical evidence, and if so, *how much* evidence do we need? Is there any room for pure reasoning or intuition – even just a hunch? Should scepticism (doubt) always be our basic position?

94

CASE STUDY: Computers and epistemology

Epistemology has proved a crucial area in the development of computer science in the last 50 years or so. Understanding how humans know things has proven crucial for:

* **computer programming** – the development of artificial logical and linguistic systems that more or less correspond to (or even improve upon) human equivalents
* **human–computer interaction** (HCI) – both software and hardware have to work with (and not against) the way human users acquire knowledge.

In turn, computers have influenced epistemology. By using computers as a 'transparent' model for the **human brain**, researchers can seek to deepen our knowledge of how we 'know'.

9 Ethics

Right and wrong

What makes an act good, what bad?

Ancient man, as well as wondering about the origins of the world about him, also sought to find moral codes and principles that would help society to flourish. Such early forms of ethics were often rooted in **reciprocity** – the Golden Rule. Early on morality became entangled with **religion** (e.g. the Ten Commandments) or graduated to the status of **laws** (e.g. the Mesopotamian Code of Hammurabi).

Ever since the ancient Greeks, philosophers have tried to find rational bases for the development of ethics and to refine the concept of right and wrong. What makes an act good, what bad? Is it something intrinsic to the act itself, or does it lie in the intention of the doer – the moral agent?

In this chapter we will look at:

* the **three main approaches** in ethics: consequentialism, virtue ethics, and deontology
* **utilitarianism** – the 'greatest happiness' principle
* **applied ethics**, with a closer look at the concept of the 'just war'.

● 'The Golden Rule of reciprocity… yeah, right!'

Making moral judgements

What are the criteria by which we should judge the morality of an act? Very broadly there are three main systems or approaches:

1 consequentialism
2 virtue ethics
3 deontology (discussed in the following section).

Consequentialism

* In this view the moral worth of an act is judged entirely on its **outcome**: e.g. telling a lie is bad because it breaks down trust.
* One obvious **objection** to consequentialism is that, morally speaking, it separates the act, and indeed the agent (the doer of the act), from the consequences of the act – an outcome might be good but the act 'bad', and vice versa:
  e.g. a lie might be good because it spares someone's feelings.
* Since we can only loosely predict the outcome of any particular act,

the act is drained of any moral content and, since their intention counts for nothing, the agent is **absolved** of moral responsibility.

Virtue ethics

* While consequentialism emphasizes outcomes, virtue ethics emphasizes the **temperament of the agent**.
* In this view what makes an act good is how the agent responds to a particular set of circumstances and deploys their inner qualities – their **virtues** – in a pragmatic way.
* The agent has the responsibility for nurturing their virtues, and the best way to do this is by **practising** and **reflecting on the nature** of these virtues (as in the early dialogues of Plato).

The Golden Mean
For Aristotle, and indeed many other ancient thinkers, virtue could often be achieved by following a 'middle way' between two vices. For example, courage was the middle way between foolhardiness and cowardice.

Deontology

* Deontological ethics insist that morality is not based primarily on either outcomes or the agent's virtues but on **rules** or **duties**. (The first part of the word deontology derives from the Greek word *dei*, meaning 'I must'.)

* In this viewpoint it is the **act** itself that takes centre stage – it's wrong to lie and that's that! The Ten Commandments represent an especially absolutist take on deontology.

* Some deontologists argue that rules act as a kind of brake, or constraint, on our actions:
  e.g. killing is always wrong – it would even be wrong to kill to save two other people being killed (such an act might be acceptable according to the consequentialist view).

'Thou shalt not kill.'
The Ten Commandments

102

What makes a rule right?

A major problem with deontology is deciding on what basis we should determine whether a rule is right. Do we simply take it at face value (hardly a philosophical stance) or do we look for some underlying well-reasoned principle?

One possible solution is the famous **Golden Rule**, often used as the basis for the ethical codes of ancient societies. In ancient Egypt it was phrased thus: 'Do to the doer to cause that he do'; and in the Christian New Testament, 'And as ye would that men should do to you, do ye also to them likewise'.

Kant came up with a more strictly rational justification for deontology – the **categorical imperative** (discussed in Chapter 4).

Utilitarianism

Utilitarianism argues that the morality of an act should be judged by its ability to produce the greatest happiness. It thus combines **consequentialism**, which emphasizes the importance of outcomes, with **hedonism** – the pursuit of pleasure as the greatest good.

Utilitarianism's best-known exponent is the English philosopher **Jeremy Bentham** (1748–1832), who used it as a basis for arguing for all kinds of social reforms – from the abolition of slavery to the decriminalization of homosexuality and animal rights.

'Nature has placed mankind under the governance of two sovereign masters, pain and pleasure.'

Jeremy Bentham

Utilitarianism has been enormously influential in the development of the modern liberal state as well as consumerist capitalism.

104

CASE STUDY: Animal rights

Philosophers before Bentham **excluded animals** as a subject for moral deliberation:

* Descartes argued that animals were **machines** and had no feelings
* Kant argued that, unlike humans, they were **not ends in themselves** and therefore had no rights – we should only be kind to them as a kind of training ground for being kind to other humans!
* Bentham was the first major philosopher to espouse animal rights – on the utilitarian argument they felt **pain** and that this should be minimized
* only in the late twentieth century were Bentham's ideas more widely taken up, as philosophers like the Australian Peter Singer (1946–) began to the question the **anthropocentrism** and **speciesism** of traditional ethics.

Applied ethics

So far we have been dealing largely with **theoretical** ethics, which deals with something like moral 'first principles'. However, unsurprisingly a large part of ethics deals with its application to everyday life – not just to our personal choices and values but also to professions and other societal fields of activity (see Figure 9.1 for some examples).

Figure 9.1: Ethics applies to all aspects of everyday life

It can be argued that the flourishing of applied ethics is vital for a **healthy society**, one that is prepared to reflect upon, question and adapt its values.

CASE STUDY: The just war

Can war be morally justified? Taking the deontological viewpoint, if we recognize that it is wrong to kill, how can it ever be right to take life?

This was the dilemma faced by the late Roman Empire, which had adopted Christianity as its state religion: for Christians, killing was morally repugnant but they quickly realized that being prepared to fight was necessary if the empire was going to survive.

To square this particular circle, St Augustine came up with the idea of the 'just war'. To be just, a war:

* had to have a **just cause** (e.g. self-defence, the punishment of wrongdoers)
* had to be waged only in the **last resort**
* had to be undertaken by a legitimate authority (e.g. by the will of a parliament).

10 How to do philosophy

Philosophical skills

Good, clear thinking – at least of the kind usually used in philosophy – consists of mental processes such as:

* **reasoning**
* **reflecting**
* **calculating**

all of which, of course, are dependent on **language**.

Philosophy – the art of thinking, to put it one way, or higher-order thinking, to put in another – is dependent on an ability to do all these things well – unambiguously, effectively and efficiently as possible; and in such a way as to be able to **communicate** to others the path you have taken.

Clear thought and communication are both vital to philosophy.

In this chapter we will look at:

* **dialectic** – a kind of philosophical dialogue that leads (hopefully) towards the truth
* **logic** – the formal principles of reasoning
* **language** – as a tool or hindrance in the pursuit of philosophical truths.

Finally, we'll look at how *you* can do philosophy – and not just leave it to the academics and the 'great thinkers' of the past.

Clear thought and communication are both vital to philosophy

Dialectic

Dialectic was one of the dominant methods of philosophizing for thousands of years:

* In essence, dialectic was a **conversation** (Greek: *dialektos*) that sought to seek out the truth of a subject through an exchange of differing viewpoints. As the discussion progressed, the two views would move towards a **synthesis** or resolution. It is notable, however, that in Plato's Socratic dialogues such a resolution is never really reached… the truth is always just out of our grasp!

* There was also a strong tradition of dialectic in ancient India, where philosophical exchanges were conducted as a form of courtly entertainment. The adoption of **multiple viewpoints** reflected the key epistemological idea of Indian philosophy that truth was infinite and therefore ultimately unobtainable by finite human beings.

* Although Christianity claimed to possess the truth, dialectic also featured in medieval Christendom in scholarly disputes between learned churchmen. St Augustine approved of dialectic because he

112

believed it could **deepen knowledge** of the faith; others argued that it led to heresy. The practice of dialectic, associated with the 'obscure' argumentation of the scholastics, died out at the end of the Middle Ages, and philosophy became a more individual pursuit.

● Modern dialectics…

Logic

As we've seen, **Aristotle** was the pioneer of the use of logic (reasoning) in philosophy and Aristotelian logic remained influential right until the closing decades of the nineteenth century. Classical logic differentiates between:

1 inductive *and*
2 deductive reasoning.

Inductive reasoning (induction) proceeds from a particular case to a general theory, for example:

* all known planets orbit the Sun in an elliptical orbit
* therefore *all* planets orbit around all stars in an elliptical orbit.

This is the reasoning used in **science**. However, most philosophers consider it flawed as a basis for philosophical thought. This is generally because it relies on human experience, which is necessarily limited by the parameters of time and space – it's possible, for all we know, that in the future nature may change dramatically (Hume's argument).

Philosophers are (or used to be) generally much happier with **deductive reasoning**, under which a conclusion follows necessarily from a given set of premises. We've met this before in the discussion of Aristotelian syllogisms, but here's another example as a reminder:

* all dogs are mammals
* all mammals have hearts
* therefore all dogs have hearts.

This is 'pure reason' – dependent not on experience but a kind of internal, even mathematical logic. As Aristotle realized, however, such reasoning could be valid logically but nonetheless not true. For example:

* *if* all men are immortal
* *and* Socrates is a man
* *then* Socrates is immortal.

Needless to say, since modern times Aristotelian logic has been subjected to a great deal of philosophical pummelling.

Language

Before the twentieth century, philosophers largely put their trust in language as a means of expressing and developing thought. Indeed, the formal logic developed from Aristotle depended on a certain **transparency** of language – words related in a more or less direct way with corresponding concepts in our heads and objects in the real world (see Figure 10.1).

While it was recognized that language could be a treacherous, deceptive thing, a good philosopher always aimed to shape it to allow his thought to shine through.

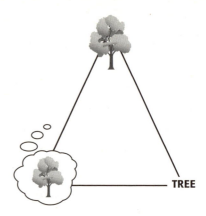

TREE

Figure 10.1: The old-school transparency of language

116

Faith in language as a kind of philosophical scalpel was already being eroded in the nineteenth century, but was blown apart by the Swiss linguist Ferdinand de Saussure (1857–1913). In his posthumous *Course in General Linguistics* (1916) he argued that:

✳ the relationship between words, concepts and things was much more **arbitrary** than had hitherto been assumed
✳ language structured or even constituted reality and anything beyond language was literally **inconceivable**.

Such ideas were a powerful influence on Wittgenstein, who in his *Tractatus Logico-Philosophicus* concluded:

> *What we cannot speak about we must pass over in silence.*

With this oracular phrase he signalled a **wholesale retreat of philosophy** from the metaphysical and into the world of language.

Do attempt to do this at home!

Philosophy need not be merely an academic discipline, the preserve of scholars and bookworms. As we've seen, its origins lie in something at once much more ordinary and extraordinary – our wonder in the everyday world around us. Philosophy is something that comes naturally to us – it's wired into our brains. Children cannot stop themselves from asking questions, as every parent knows. As adults, however, we somehow lose the habit, lose our capacity for wonder.

118

Here's my advice if you want to start philosophizing:

* Start **reading** a few of the philosophers you've come across in this book – they're not half so scary as they seem! See the Further Reading section for some pointers.
* Try to rediscover **your philosophical bent of mind** – read slowly, give yourself time and space to think, jot down your thoughts, and above all keep **your eyes open** (both literally and metaphorically).

✳ If you don't think it's too precious, join or start a **philosophy club** – start with simple questions, exchange ideas, challenge them (politely)…

In the introduction to this book I described a view of philosophy – the kind portrayed by Plato in his dialogues – that was:

✳ useful
✳ sociable
✳ humane *and*
✳ enjoyable.

I hope that as you've read through this book you have discovered that philosophy has the potential to be all these things.

● A modern symposium…

Further reading

As I suggested at the beginning of this book the best place to start reading the great philosophers is Plato. No one else captures better the sheer intellectual excitement and passion of philosophy nor does so in quite as entertaining a way. Try the *Symposium* or the *Phaedo* or, if you're feeling a little braver, the *Republic*. Here's a handful of other texts that I would recommend:

* Aristotle, *Nicomachean Ethics*
* Camus, Albert, *The Myth of Sisyphus*
* Descartes, René, *Metaphysical Meditations*
* *The First Philosophers: The Presocratics and Sophists* (Oxford World's Classics)
* Hume, David, *A Treatise of Human Nature*
* Nietzsche, Friedrich, *Human, All Too Human*
* Sartre, Jean-Paul, *Existentialism is a Humanism*
* Wittgenstein, Ludwig, *Tractatus Logico-Philosophicus*